D1794694

1

2

3

NAME THE NAME OF JESUS.

By

John C Burt.

4

Photographs Courtesy of :

philippe - awouters.

jason - betz.

birmingham - museums - trust.

edward - cisneros.

edwin - andrade.

bruno - martins.

Free Downloads on :

unsplash.com

5

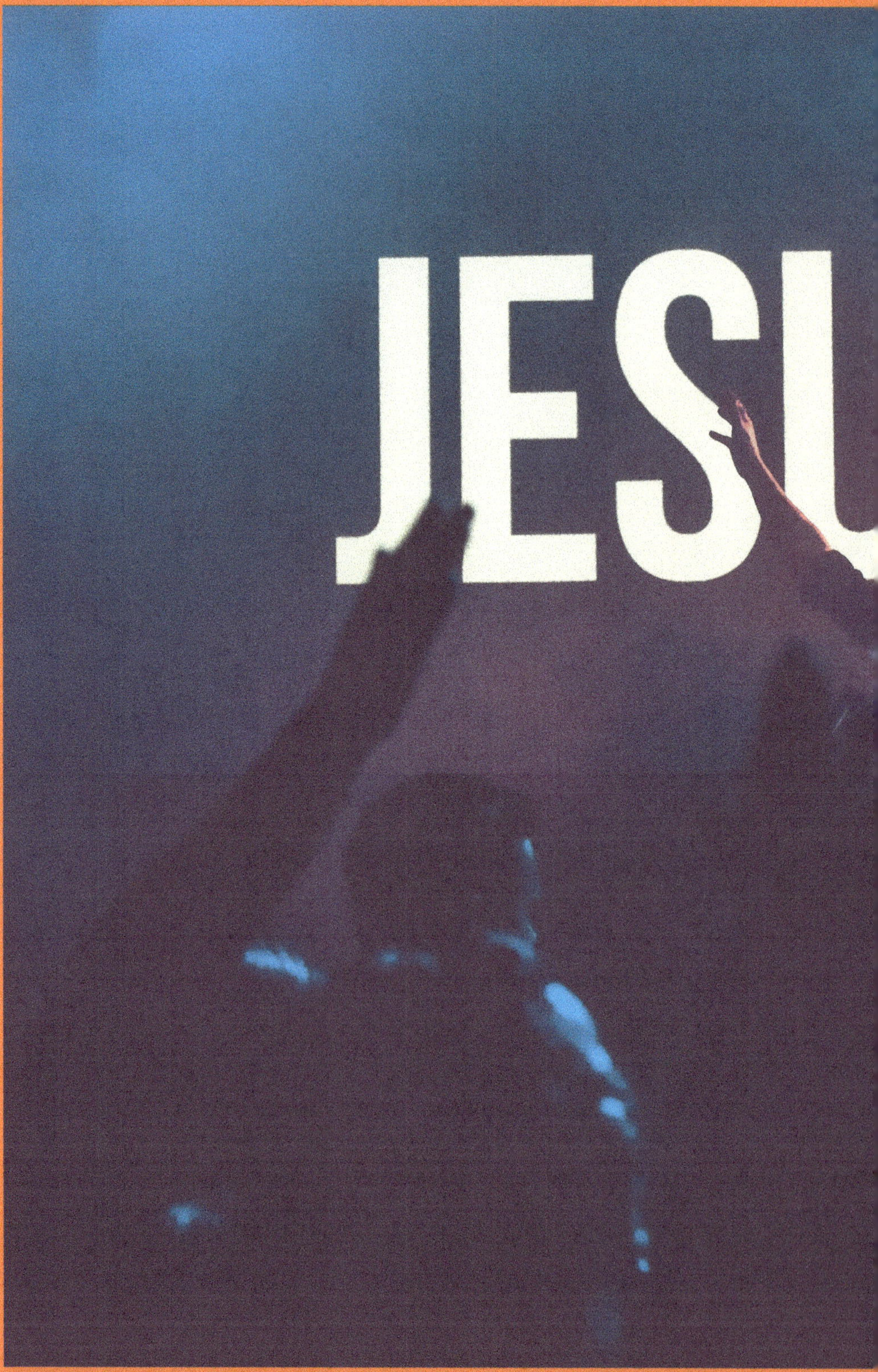
JESU

FOREWORD :

I am sitting here writing this very book and I am struck by the very reality of the very real power and authority behind the Name of the Lord Jesus Christ? This ...

Name when it is invoked has the power to change lives, situations and circumstances? May well be ,

20

that you have never thought too much about it? But the very Name of Jesus is powerful and can , will and ..

does change
everything for
the better when
it is invoked
and let loose
over lives and
circumstances!

22

In this very book I want to think about the various Names of the Lord Jesus Christ; the Names He goes by in the Word of God; the New Testament primarily. To seek to understand the diamond that is the Lord Jesus Christ; one needs to seek to see it from different angles and perspectives?

Seeking to understand the Diamond that is the Lord Jesus Christ by looking at One Name will not

26

work. We need to consider the many names of the Lord Jesus Christ to even try to begin to understand Him!

27

To do this well
we consider
some of the
relevant texts
to do with the
various Names
of the Lord ...
28

Jesus Christ from the Word of God. We will then discuss the implications of each Name of Jesus Christ?

29

30

31

32

33

34

36

37

38

39

40

41

1.

Starting from this chapter onwards we will be citing the Word of God. The relevant Scriptures

to do with the various Names of the Lord Jesus Christ? There will be three different versions of the texts given; they are the ESV, the NIV and the GNT translations of the texts.

{ ESV }

LORD :

MATTHEW 7 : 21.

44

" (21) " Not everyone who says to me, ' Lord, Lord,' will enter the kingdom of heaven, but the one who does the will of my Father who is in heaven." "

MARK 12 : 29.

45

" (29) Jesus answered, " The most important is, ' Hear, O Israel: The Lord our God, the Lord is one. "

LUKE 6 : 46.

" (46) " Why do you call me ' Lord, Lord,' and not do what I tell you? ""

LUKE 24 : 34.

" (34) saying, " The Lord has risen indeed, and has appeared to Simon! " "

ACTS 10 : 36.

" (36) As for the word that he sent to Israel, preaching good news of peace through

Jesus Christ (he is Lord of all), ""

JESUS :

ACTS 2 : 32.

" (32) This Jesus God raised up, and of that we all are witnesses. "

48

ACTS 9 : 5.

" (5) And he said, "Who are you, Lord?" and he said, " 1 am Jesus, whom you are persecuting." "

ACTS 9 : 33 - 34.

" (33) There he found a man named Aeneas, bedridden for eight years, who was paralyzed.

(34) And Peter said to him, " Aeneas, Jesus Christ heals you; rise and make your bed.""

50

ROMANS 3 : 24.

" (24) and are justified by his grace as a gift, through the redemption that is in Christ Jesus, "

ROMANS 5 : 17.

" (17) For if, because of one man's trespass, death reigned through that one man, much more will those who receive the abundance of grace and the free gift of righteousness reign in life through the one man Jesus Christ. "

ROMANS 8 : 1.

" (1) There is therefore now no condemnation for those who are in Christ Jesus."

1 CORINTHIANS 2 : 2.

" (2) For 1
decided to know nothing
among you except Jesus
Christ and him crucified."

CHRIST :

MATTHEW 1 :
16.

54

" (16) and Jacob the father of Joseph the husband of Mary, of whom Jesus was born, who is called Christ."

MATTHEW 22 : 42.

" (42) saying, " What do you think about the Christ? Whose son is he?" They said to him,

" The son of David." "

MARK 1 : 1.

" (1) The beginning of the gospel of Jesus Christ, the Son of God."

MARK 8 : 29.

56

" (29) And he asked them, " But who do you say the 1 am?" Peter answered him, " You are the Christ." "

MARK 14 : 61.

" (61) But he remained silent and made no answer. Again the high priest asked him, " Are you the Christ,

the Son of the
Blessed?""

LUKE 9 : 20.

" (20) Then he
said to them, " But who
do you say that 1 am?"
And Peter answered,
" The Christ of God.""

JOHN 20 : 30 - 31.

" (30) Now Jesus did many other signs in the presence of the disciples, which are not written in this book;

(31) but these are written so that you may believe that Jesus is the Christ, the Son of God,

and that by believing you may have life in his name."

ACTS 2 : 36.

" (36) Let all the house of Israel therefore know for certain that God has made him both Lord and Christ, this Jesus whom you crucified." "

60

ACTS 5 : 42.

" (42) And every day, in the temple and from house to house, they did not cease teaching and preaching that Christ is Jesus."

SON OF

GOD :

MATTHEW 4: 3.

" (3) And the tempter came and said to him, " If you are the Son of God, command

62

these stones to become loaves of bread. " "

MATTHEW 14 : 33.

" (33) And those in the boat worshiped him, saying, " Truly you are the Son of God." "

MATTHEW 27 : 54.

" (54) When the centurion and those who were with him, keeping watch over Jesus, saw the earthquake and what took place, they were filled with awe and said, " Truly this was the Son of God! " "

JOHN 11 : 4.

" (4) But when Jesus heard it he said, " This illness does not lead to death. It is for the glory of God, so that the Son of God may be glorified through it." "

LAMB OF GOD:

JOHN 1 : 29.

" (29) The next day he saw Jesus coming toward him, and

66

said, " Behold, the Lamb
of God, who takes away
the sin of the world! "

SON OF
MAN :

MATTHEW 8 :
20.

" (20) And Jesus said to him, " Foxes have holes, and birds of the air have nests, but the Son of Man has nowhere to lay his head." "

MATTHEW 12 : 8.

" (8)" For the Son of Man is lord of the Sabbath." "

MATTHEW 12 : 32.

" (32) And whoever speaks a word against the Son of Man will be forgiven, but whoever speaks against the Holy Spirit will not be forgiven, either in this age or in the age to come." "

MATTHEW 12 : 40.

" (40) For just as Jonah was three days and three nights in the

belly of the great fish,
so will the Son of Man
be three days and three
nights in the heart of
the earth." "

MARK 2 : 28.

" (28) "So the Son
of Man is lord even of
the Sabbath." "

MATTHEW 8 : 38.

" (38) For whoever is ashamed of me and of my words in this adulterous and sinful generation, of him will the Son of Man also be ashamed when he comes in the glory of his Father with the holy angels." "

LUKE 9 : 58.

" (58) And Jesus said to him, " Foxes have holes, and birds of the air have nests, but the Son of Man has nowhere to lay his head." "

LUKE 19 : 10.

" (10)" For the Son of Man came to seek and to save the lost." "

JOHN 3 : 14 - 15.

74

" (14) "And as Moses lifted up the serpent in the wilderness, so must the Son of Man be lifted up,

(15) that whoever believes in him may have eternal life." "

MESSIAH:

JOHN 1 : 41.

" (41) He first found his own brother Simon and said to him, " We have found the Messiah" (which means

76

Christ)." "

JOHN 4 : 25 – 26.

" (25) The woman said to him, " 1 know that Messiah is coming (he who is called Christ). When he comes, he will tell us all things.

(26) Jesus said to her, " I who speak to you am he." "

' I AM ' STATEMENTS IN JOHN'S GOSPEL :

78

JOHN 6 : 35.

" (35) Jesus said to them, " I am the bread of life; whoever comes to me shall not hunger, and whoever believes in me shall never thirst." "

JOHN 8 : 12.

" (12) Again Jesus spoke to them, saying, " I am the light of the world. Whoever follows me will not walk in darkness, but will have the light of life." "

JOHN 10 : 7.

" (7) So Jesus again said to them, " Truly, truly, I say to you, I am the door of the sheep" "

JOHN 10 : 11.

" (11)" I am the good shepherd. The good shepherd lays down his life for the sheep""

JOHN 11 : 25 - 26.

" (25) Jesus said to her, " 1 am the resurrection and the life. Whoever believes in me, though he die, yet shall he live,

(26) and everyone who lives and

believes in me shall never die. Do you believe this? " "

JOHN 14 : 6.

" (6) Jesus said to him, " I am the way, the truth, and the life. No one comes to the Father except through me. " "

JOHN 15 : 1 , 5.

" (1) " 1 am the true vine, and my father is the vine-dresser. " "

(5) 1 am the vine; you are the branches. Whoever abides in me and 1 in him, he it is that bears much fruit, for apart from

84

me you can do
nothing." "

86

87

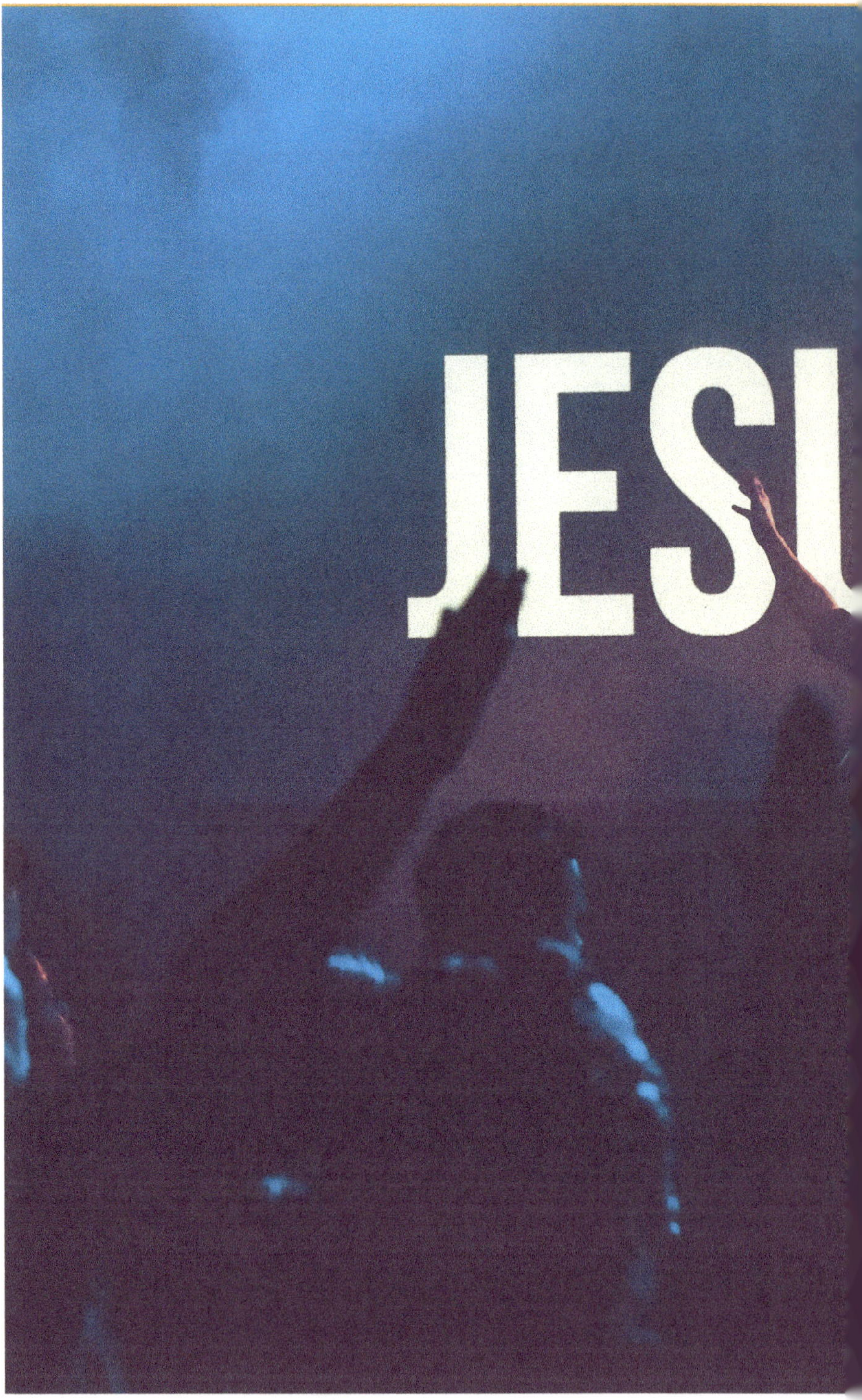
JESU

90

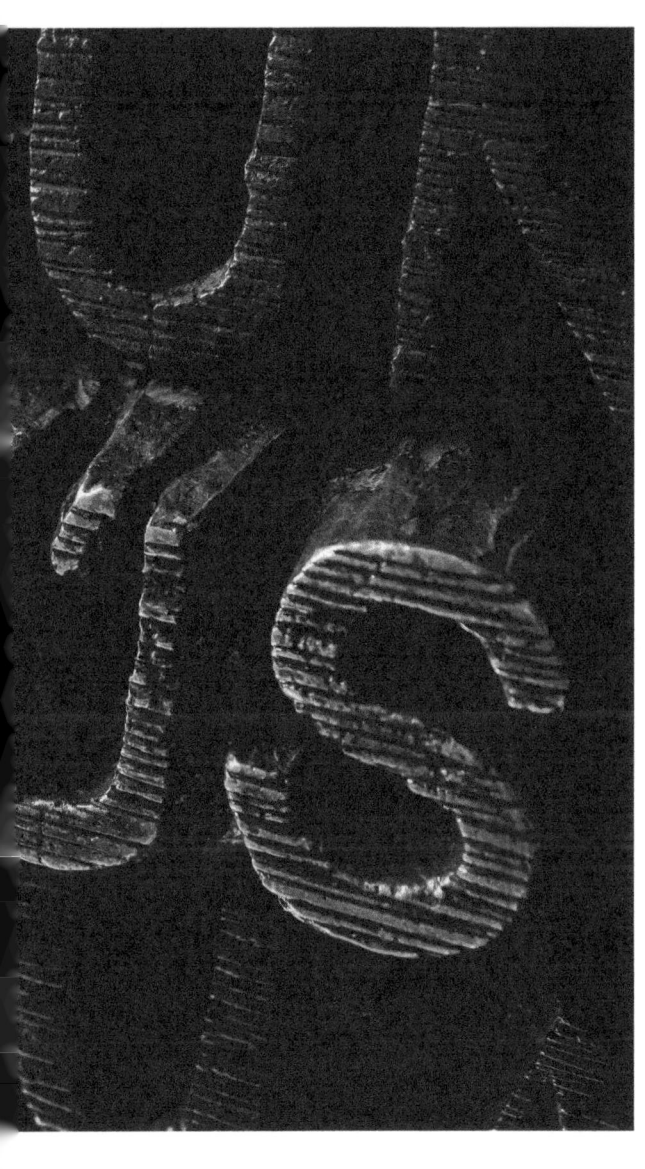

91

93

94

ATHAWAY

STEVEN

T WISH

LER

95

97

2.

{ NIV }

LORD :

MATTHEW 7 : 21.

" (21) " Not everyone who says to me, ' Lord, Lord,' will enter the kingdom of heaven, but only the one who does the will of my Father who is in heaven. " "

MARK 12 : 29.

" (29) " The most important one," answered Jesus, " is this: ' Hear, O Israel: The Lord our God, the Lord is one.""

LUKE 6 : 46.

100

" (46) " Why do you call me, ' Lord,Lord,' and do not do what i say? "

LUKE 24 : 34.

" (34) and saying, " It is true! The Lord has risen and has appeared to Simon." "

ACTS 10 : 36.

" (36) "You know the message God sent to the people of Israel, announcing the good news of peace through Jesus Christ, who is Lord of all." "

102

JESUS :

ACTS 2 : 32.

" (32)" God has raised this Jesus to life, and we are all witnesses of it.""

ACTS 9 : 5.

" (5) " Who are you, Lord?" Saul asked. " I am Jesus, who you are persecuting," he replied." "

ACTS 9 : 33 - 34.

104

" (33) There he found a man named Aeneas, who was paralyzed and had been bedridden for eight years.

(34) " Aeneas," Peter said to him, " Jesus Christ heals you. Get up and roll up your mat." Immediately Aeneas got up" "

ROMANS 3 : 24.

" (24) and all are justified freely by his grace through the redemption that came by Christ Jesus. "

ROMANS 5 : 17.

106

" (17) For if, by the trespass of the one man, death reigned through that one man, how much more will those who receive God's abundant provision of grace and the gift of righteousness reign in life through the one man, Jesus Christ! "

ROMANS 8 : 1.

" (1) Therefore, there is now no condemnation for those who are in Christ Jesus,"

1 CORINTHIANS

2 : 2

" (2) For 1 resolved to know nothing while 1 was with you except Jesus Christ and him crucified."

CHRIST :

MATTHEW 1 : 16.

" (16) and Jacob the father of Joseph, the husband of Mary, and Mary was the mother of Jesus who is called the Messiah."

MATTHEW 22 : 42.

"(42) " What do you think about the Messiah? Whose son is he? "

" The son of David," they replied.""

MARK 1 : 1.

" (1) The beginning of the good news about Jesus the Messiah, the Son of God, "

MARK 8 : 29.

112

"(29) " But what about you? " he asked. " Who do you say I am?"

Peter answered, " You are the Messiah.""

MARK 14 : 61.

" (61) But Jesus remained silent and gave no answer.

Again the high priest asked him, " Are you the Messiah, the Son of the Blessed One?""

LUKE 9 : 20.

114

" (20) " But what about you?" he asked. " Who do you say I am?"

Peter answered,
" God's Messiah." "

JOHN 20 : 30 - 31.

" (30) Jesus performed many other signs in the presence of his disciples, which are not recorded in this book. (31) But these are written that you may believe that Jesus is the Messiah, the Son of God, and that by believing you may have life in his name. " "

ACTS 2 : 36.

" (36) " Therefore let all Israel be assured of this: God has made this Jesus, whom you crucified, both Lord and Messiah." "

ACTS 5 : 42.

" (42) Day after day, in the temple courts and from house to house, they never stopped teaching and proclaiming the good news that Jesus is the Messiah." "

SON OF GOD :

MATTHEW 4 : 3.

" (3) The tempter came to him and said, " If you are the Son of

God, tell these stones to become bread." "

MATTHEW 14 : 33.

" (33) Then those who were in the boat worshiped him, saying, " Truly you are the Son of God." "

120

" (54) When the centurion and those with him who were guarding Jesus saw the earthquake and all that had happened, they were terrified, and exclaimed, " Surely he was the Son of God! " "

LAMB OF

GOD :

JOHN 1 : 29.

" (29) The next day John saw Jesus coming toward him and said, " Look, the Lamb

122

of God, who takes away
the sin of the world! ""

SON OF
MAN :

MATTHEW 8 : 20.

" (20) Jesus replied, " Foxes have dens and birds have nests, but the Son of Man has no place to lay his head." "

MATTHEW 12 : 8.

" (8) For the Son of Man is the Lord of the Sabbath. " "

MATTHEW 12 : 32.

" (32) Anyone who speaks a word against the Son of Man will be forgiven, but anyone who speaks against the Holy Spirit will not be forgiven, either in this age or in the age to come. " "

MATTHEW 12 : 40.

" (40) For as Jonah was three days and three nights in the belly of a huge fish, so the Son of Man will be three days and three nights in the heart of the earth. " "

MARK 2 : 28.

" (28) " So the Son of Man is Lord even of the Sabbath." "

MARK 8 : 38.

128

" (38) "If anyone is ashamed of me and my words in this adulterous and sinful generation, the Son of Man will be ashamed of them when he comes in his Father's glory with the holy angels." "

LUKE 9 : 58.

" (58) Jesus replied, " Foxes have dens and birds have nests, but the Son of Man has no place to lay his head." "

LUKE 19 : 10.

" (10)" For the Son of Man came to seek and to save the lost." "

JOHN 3 : 14 – 15.

" (14) Just as Moses lifted up the snake in the wilderness, so the Son of Man must be lifted up,

(15) that everyone who believes may have eternal life in him." "

MESSIAH:

JOHN 1 : 41.

" (41) The first
thing Andrew did was to
find his brother Simon
and tell him, " We have
found the Messiah"
(that is, the Christ)." "

JOHN 4 : 25 - 26.

" (25) The woman said, " I know that Messiah" (called Christ) " is coming. When he comes, he will explain everything to us."

(26) Then Jesus

134

declared, " 1 , the one speaking to you - 1 am he." "

" I AM " STATEMENTS IN THE GOSPEL OF JOHN :

JOHN 6 : 35.

" (35) Then Jesus declared, " I am the bread of life. Whoever comes to me will never go hungry, and whoever believes in me will never be thirsty." "

JOHN 8 : 12.

" (12) When Jesus spoke again to the people, he said, " I am the light of the world. Whoever follows me will never walk in darkness, but will have the light of life." "

JOHN 10 : 7.

" (7) Therefore Jesus said again, " Very truly 1 tell you, 1 am the gate for the sheep" "

JOHN 10 : 11.

138

" (11) " 1 am the good shepherd. The good shepherd lays down his life for the sheep." "

JOHN 11 : 25 – 26.

" (25) Jesus said to her, " 1 am the resurrection and the life. The one who believes in me will live, even though they die;

(26) and whoever lives by believing in me will never die. Do you believe this? " "

JOHN 14 : 6.

140

" (6) Jesus answered, " I am the way and the truth and the life. No one comes to the Father except through me." "

JOHN 15 : 1 , 5.

" (1) " I am the true vine, and my Father is the gardener. " "

" (5) " I am the vine; you are the branches. If you remain in me and I in you, you will bear much fruit; apart from me you can do nothing." "

143

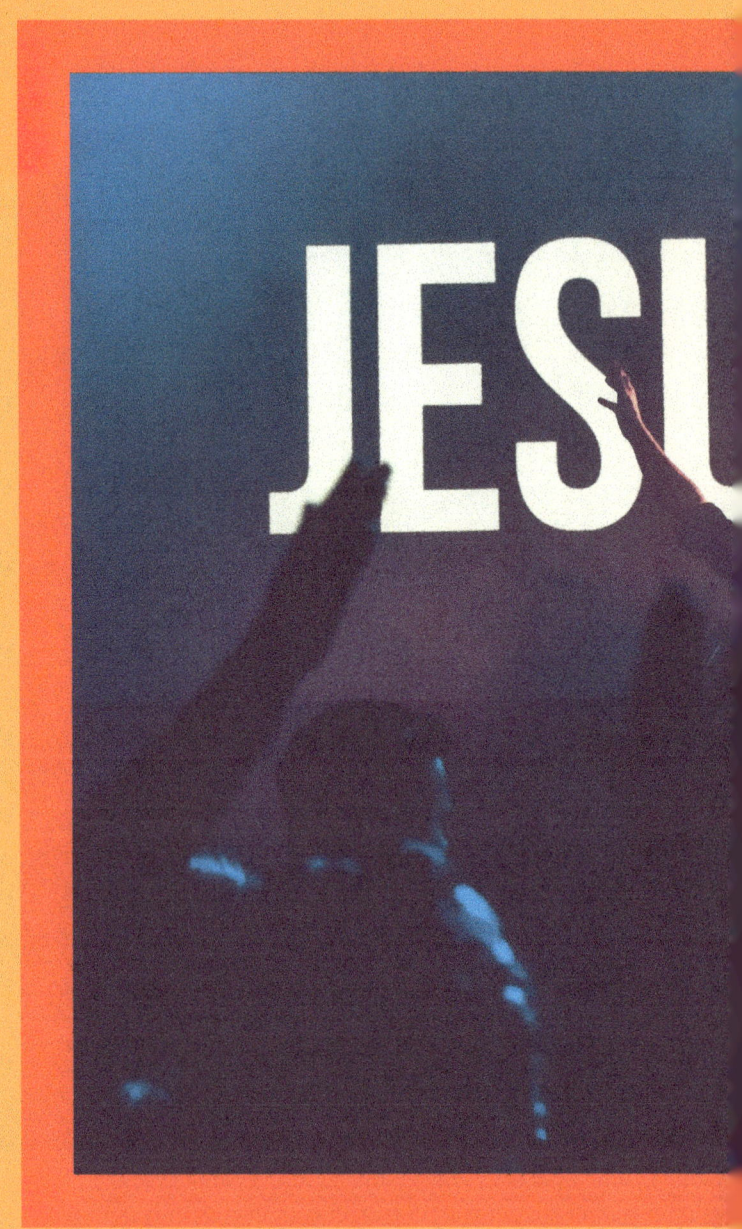

144

145

149

3.

{ GNT }

LORD :

150

MATTHEW 7 : 21.

" (21) " Not everyone who calls me 'Lord, Lord' will enter the Kingdom of heaven, but only those who do what my Father in heaven wants them to do." "

MARK 12 : 29.

" (29) Jesus replied, " The most important one is this : ' Listen, Israel! The Lord our God is the only Lord.' " "

LUKE 6 : 46.

" (46) " Why do you call me, ' Lord, Lord', and yet don't do what I tell you? ""

LUKE 24 : 34.

" (34) and saying, " The Lord is risen indeed! He has appeared to Simon ! " "

ACTS 10 : 36.

" (36) You know the message he sent to the people of Israel, proclaiming the Good News of peace through Jesus Christ, who is Lord of all." "

JESUS :

ACTS 2 : 32.

" (32) "God has raised this very Jesus from death, and we are all witnesses to this fact. " "

ACTS 9 : 5.

" (5) " Who are you, Lord?" he asked. " I am Jesus, whom you persecute," the voice said. " "

ACTS 9 : 33 - 34.

156

" (33) There he met a man named Aeneas, who was paralyzed and had not been able to get out of bed for eight years.
(34) " Aeneas," Peter said to him, " Jesus Christ makes you well. Get up and make your bed." At once Aeneas got up" "

ROMANS 3 : 24.

" (24) But by the free gift of God's grace all are put right with him through Christ Jesus, who sets them free. " "

ROMANS 5 : 17.

" (17) It is true that through the sin of one man death began to rule because of that one man. But how much greater is the result of what was done by the one man, Jesus Christ! All who receive God' abundant

grace and are freely put
right with him will rule
in life through Christ.""

ROMANS 8 : 1.

" (1) "There is no
condemnation now for
those who live in union
with Christ Jesus." "

1 CORINTHIANS 2 : 2.

" (2) For while 1 was with you, 1 made up my mind to forget everything except Jesus Christ and especially his death on the cross. " "

CHRIST :

MATTHEW 1 : 16.

" (16) ..... Jacob, and Joseph, who married Mary, the mother of Jesus , who was called

162

the Messiah." "

MATTHEW 22 : 42.

" (42) " What do you think about the Messiah? Whose descendant is he?

" He is David's descendant," they answered." "

MARK 1 : 1.

" (1) This is the Good News about Jesus Christ, the Son of God.""

MARK 8 : 29.

" (29) " What about you? " he asked them. " Who do you say I am?"

Peter answered, " You are the Messiah.""

MARK 14 : 61.

" (61) But Jesus kept quiet and would not say a word. Again the High Priest questioned him, " Are you the Messiah, the Son of the Blessed God?" "

LUKE 9 : 20.

" (20) " What about you?" he asked them. " Who do you say that 1 am? "
Peter answered, " You are God's Messiah." "

JOHN 20 : 30 - 31.

" (30) In his disciples' presence Jesus performed many other miracles which are not written down in this book.

(31) But these have been written in ...

168

order that you may believe that Jesus is the Messiah, the Son of God, and that through your faith in him you may have life. " "

ACTS 2 : 36.

" (36) " All the people of Israel, then, are to know for sure that this Jesus, whom you crucified, is the one that God has made Lord and Messiah ! " "

ACTS 5 : 42.

" (42) And every day in the Temple and in people's homes they continued to teach

170

and preach the Good
News about Jesus the
Messiah." "

SON OF

GOD :

MATTHEW 4 : 3.

" (3) Then the Devil came to him and said, " If you are God's Son, order these stones to turn into bread." "

MATTHEW 14 : 33.

" (33) Then the disciples in the boat worshiped Jesus. " Truly you are the Son of God!" they exclaimed.""

MATTHEW 27 : 54.

" (54) When the army officer and the soldiers with him who were watching Jesus saw the earthquake and everything else that happened, they were terrified and said, " He really was the Son of God! " "

JOHN 11 : 4.

" (4) When Jesus heard it, he said, " The final result of this sickness will not be the death of Lazarus; this has happened in order to bring glory to God,

and it will be the means
by which the Son of God
will receive glory." "

LAMB OF

GOD :

176

JOHN 1 : 29.

" (29) The next day John saw Jesus coming to him, and said, " There is the Lamb of God, who takes away the sin of the world.! " "

SON OF MAN:

MATTHEW 8 : 20.

" (20) Jesus answered him, " Foxes

have holes, and birds have nests, but the Son of Man has no place to lie down and rest." "

MATTHEW 12 : 8.

" (8) for the Son of Man is Lord of the Sabbath." "

MATTHEW 12 : 32.

" (32) Anyone who says something against the Son of Man can be forgiven; but whoever says something against the Holy Spirit will not be

forgiven - now or
ever.""

MATTHEW 12 : 40.

" (40) In the
same way that Jonah
spent three days and
nights in the big fish,
so will the Son of Man

spend three days and nights in the depths of the earth." "

MARK 2 : 28.

" (28) So the Son of Man is Lord even of the Sabbath.""

MARK 8 : 38.

" (38) If you are ashamed of me and of my teaching in this godless and wicked day, then the Son of man will be ashamed of you when he comes in the glory of his Father with the holy angels.""

LUKE 9 : 58.

" (58) Jesus said to him, " Foxes have holes, and birds have nests, but the Son of Man has no place to lie down and rest." "

LUKE 19 : 10.

" (10) The Son of Man came to seek and to save the lost." "

JOHN 3 : 14 – 15.

" (14) As Moses lifted up the bronze snake on a pole in the desert, in the same way the Son of Man must be lifted up,

(15) so that everyone who believes in him may have eternal life." "

MESSIAH:

JOHN 1 : 41.

" (41) At once he found his brother Simon and told him, " We have found the Messiah." (This word means " Christ.") " "

JOHN 4 : 25 - 26.

" (25) The woman said to him, " 1 know that the Messiah will come, and when he comes, he will tell us everything."

(26) Jesus answered, " 1 am he, 1 who am talking with you." "

" I AM " STATEMENTS IN THE GOSPEL OF JOHN .

JOHN 6 : 35.

" (35) " 1 am the bread of life," Jesus told them. " Those who come to me will never be hungry; those who believe in me will never be thirsty." "

JOHN 8 : 12.

" (12) Jesus spoke to the Pharisees again. " 1 am the light of the world," he said. " Whoever follows me will have the light of life and will never walk in darkness." "

JOHN 10 : 7.

" (7) So Jesus said again, " I am telling you the truth: I am the gate for the sheep" "

JOHN 10 : 11.

" (11) " I am the good shepherd, who is willing to die for the sheep.""

JOHN 11 : 25 – 26.

" (25) Jesus said to her, " I am the resurrection and the life. Those who believe in me will live, even though they die;

(26) and those who live and believe in me will never die. Do you believe this? " "

JOHN 14 : 6.

" (6) Jesus answered him, " I am the way, the truth, and the life; no one goes to the Father except by me." "

JOHN 15 : 1 , 5.

" (1) " I am the real vine, and my Father is the gardener." "

" (5) " I am the vine, and you are the branches. Those who remain in me, and I in them, will bear much fruit; for you can do nothing without me. " "

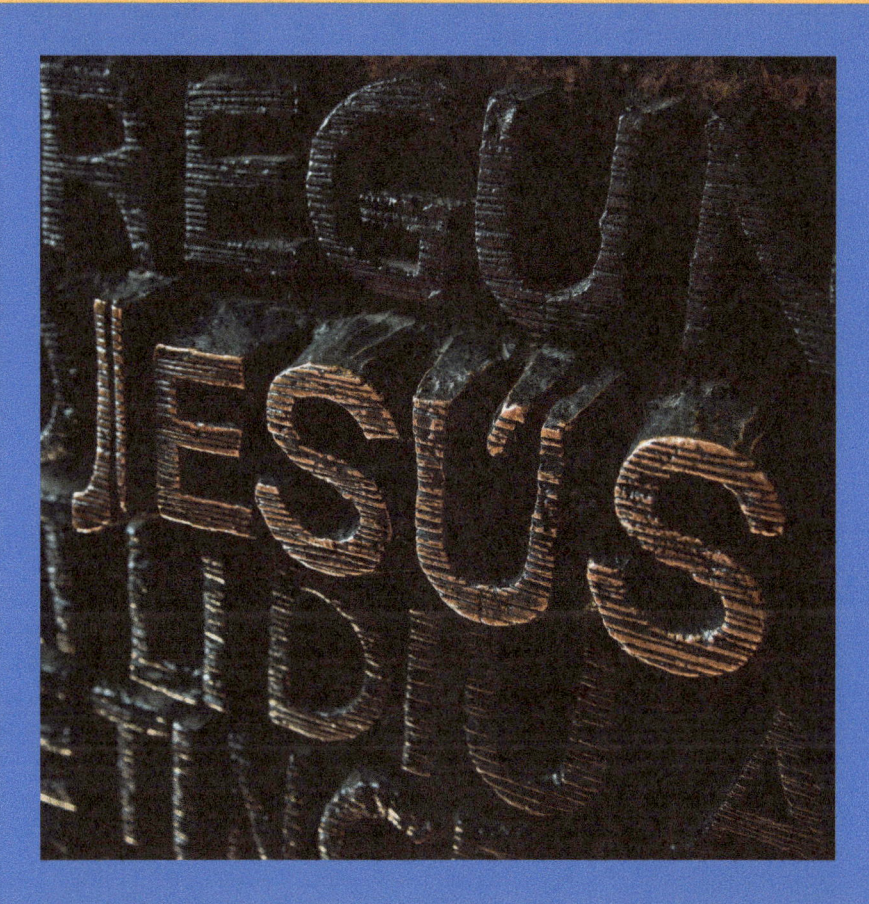

197

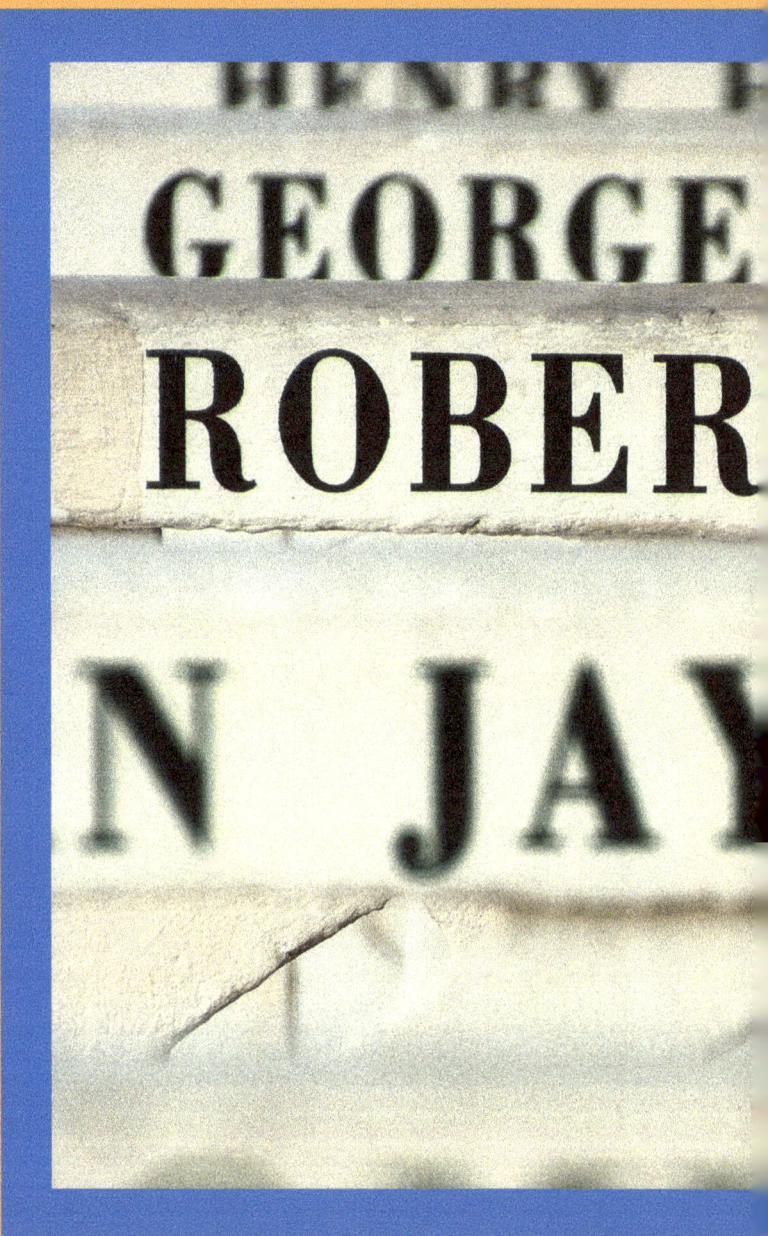

198

200

201

202

203

204

205

4.

LORD :

We will start this part of the book with a consideration of the Name of the Lord Jesus Christ as 'LORD ?' In our days, it is fashionable to talk about such things as Lordship Theology? However,

207

even this very theology does not get to the very heart of what it means for the Lord Jesus Christ to be your LORD? It's interesting, that one of the Names for the Lord God Almighty in the Old Testament was LORD. So, when this term is used of the Lord Jesus Christ ; He is being equated with the LORD GOD ALMIGHTY of the Old Testament? It's all caught up with ...

209

the divinity question that always surrounds the Lord Jesus Christ? Was He truly God or was He not? In the end, it is this very question that one has to answer for ..

themselves as they seek after the very truth about the Lord Jesus Christ. To put it simply; if He were in fact God, then we do need to take the appropriate action in our own lives and receive Him? If He was not the God He claimed to be then we can forget about Him? Therefore, the question of whether or not He was and is the 'Lord' Jesus Christ is terribly important to come to terms with !

When you
make Him LORD of
your life ; you are
ceding control of
your life to Him. All
of which is why, it is
so important what
you decide in terms
of whether or not He
was and is LORD ?

Furthermore, it is worth that in Matthew 7 : 21 having Him as LORD of your life is equated with then doing the will of the Father in your life? Because as He says not everybody who calls Him LORD - LORD has Him as their Lord ; rather it is the ones who do the will of the Father in and through their lives who really have Him as LORD. All of which fits in with other teaching

215

of His , that obedience and doing the very commands of the Lord God Almighty is much better than any sacrifice you make to Him and His Father?

It is worth noting at this juncture that

216

Names of the Lord Jesus Christ we are thinking about are in reality intertwined with each other; as one can tell from the very verses cited in this book. LORD + CHRIST = MESSIAH

217

As has been noted it is like the Lord Jesus Christ is a multi - faceted Diamond; one Name does not in any shape or form give you everything that He was and is today? Therefore, the term of LORD, while it is profound in itself does not and cannot give you the complete picture of who and is the Lord Jesus Christ, before and now today.

Finally, I want to spend some time

thinking about what the Greek word behind the word LORD means and says to us? It has the sense of 'owner, master , lord and sir?' These are the very words behind the use of the term

220

LORD by the Lord Jesus Christ in the verses cited from the New Testament. As one can see the semantic range of meaning is widespread and rather involved. So therefore the Lord

Jesus Christ is saying that He is all these things when He uses the term LORD to denote and talk about Himself in the verses cited by this book.

It is interesting

to think about the term LORD in terms of it meaning ' owner and master ?' It is then caught up with the notion of ourselves being the 'doulos'..the ' slave of the Lord Jesus Christ ?'

223

Even from this abridged look at the semantic range of the Greek word behind the word LORD; one can see that it can and does a lot of meanings attached to it . All of

which are in play
when they are used
by people in the New
Testament;
depending upon the
context of the very
verse as well. Jesus
Christ as LORD is
very important to
understand !

228

230

231

232

235

5.

JESUS :

To begin
with; it is interesting
to think about the
very reality of the
name of ' Jesus '
being shared by the
criminal '
Barabbas?' So, the

name ' Jesus ' was
a common name
amongst the Jews of
the Lord Jesus
Christ's time.

The Greek
word for ' Jesus ' ;
' Joshua ' has the
meaning of 'Yahweh

saves.' Therefore, as one can see the name ' Jesus ' or Joshua is a profound name for the Lord Jesus Christ to have? It is caught up in His very reasons for coming to the earth from the Father. So, even though the name 'Jesus ' was a common name amongst the Jews of His time and shared by the criminal 'Barabbas' it is still significant and important to come to

240

terms with?

It is also interesting to note and come to terms with the reality that the name ' Jesus ' is used in the Gospels with the other names of Him. Yet, it is in the later letters of the New Testament that things are said and done in the Name of ' Jesus ?' The Name ' Jesus ' became a powerful and profound Name for

242

the follower's of the Lord Jesus Christ. It came to denote the one whom by they were bringing healing and even preaching in the Name of. This can be seen in the Book of Acts particularly?

He may well have had the same Name as Barabbas but the Name 'Jesus' came to mean so much more and be associated with the very power of the Lord God ...

Almighty. Therefore, the Name of ' Jesus ' can be and is a powerful Name to know and to invoke and even declare over situations and circumstances in your own life and times! There is a lot of things associated with the Name ' Jesus ' and declaring and invoking it over one's life. It brings so much with it , when it is both declared and invoked over one's life and it's situations and circumstances. It is like the very presence of the Lord Jesus Christ comes into the situation's and the circumstances. At different times and moments that is all we can bring to bear over a situation or circumstance in our own lives. Yet, it is mightily effective and profound at the same time. It's like we are bringing the Lord

248

Jesus Christ into center stage and the prominence He deserves in the very situation and circumstances we are facing.

Finally, it is also important to see that the writer's of the ...

New Testament saw the One who bore the Name ' Jesus ' as being the very fulfillment of the plan of the Lord God Almighty; His Father. For them and His follower's even now

the Name ' Jesus '
was just so
significant and
important and one to
be revered and
valued highly by all
people upon the
earth.

252

253

254

255

256

257

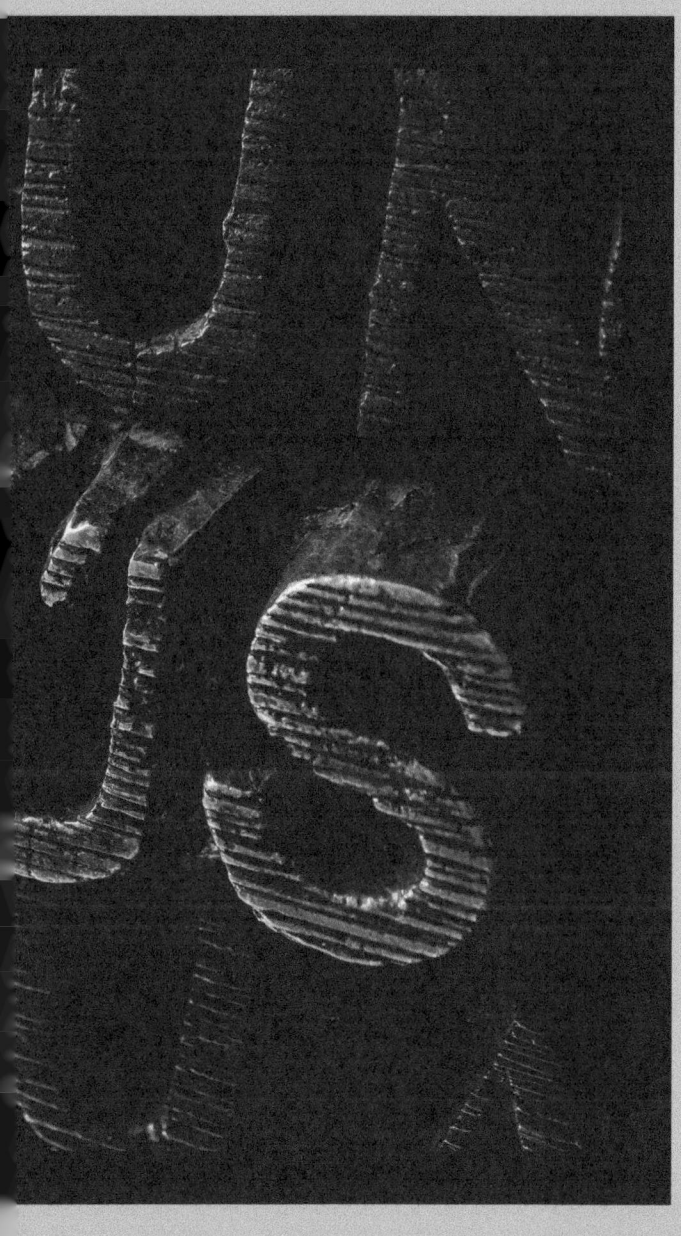

259

260

6.

CHRIST :

Matthew 1 : 16 :
{ ESV } " (16) and
Jacob the father of
Joseph the husband
of Mary, of whom
Jesus was born,
who is called
Christ."

It is very
important to come

to grips with the Name of ' Christ ?' The Greek word behind it has the meaning of anointed one or Messiah. So, as one can see this Name of the Lord Jesus Christ is so very important to our understanding of the whole of the Diamond that was the Lord Jesus Christ.

Given that He was the anointed one and the Messiah; He was the One they were awaiting from the Lord God Almighty. He was the One who was to come, the One that had been foretold about , by the Prophets of the People of the Lord God Almighty? He ..

was and is the One
they had all been
waiting for to come
from the Father.
Yet, they still did
not see this and
accept Him as the
anointed Messiah
sent from and by ..

the Father; His Father in Heaven. There were some who admittedly did receive Him as this and they were the ones who were blessed by His coming on the scene.

As the anointed one and the Messiah, the Lord Jesus Christ was part of the plan of the Father, the Lord God Almighty to reconcile humanity again to Himself. This was true for the

Jewish people and it is true for the rest of humanity. In short, Him being both the anointed one of the Lord God Almighty and the Messiah who had come was all part of the plan of the Father to rescue humanity through Him. I want to lay the stress on this reality of the Lord Jesus Christ being both the anointed One and the Messiah, because this is where the stress is in the New Testament?

271

All of which, is why it is so important when His own disciple Peter recognizes Him as the 'Christ' , the anointed One and the Messiah. The disciples and Peter in particular got so much wrong but in this regard he was on the money and correct. Therefore, not all of the people of the Jewish Faith rejected Him as the anointed One and ..

the Messiah. Peter himself would have come out of a Jewish background and out of the Jewish Faith. Therefore, which is why it is so important to our understanding of the Diamond that is and was the Lord

Jesus Christ that Peter, one of His own disciples recognizes Him as both the anointed One and the Messiah who has come to be with them as the very people of the Lord

God Almighty.

As the anointed One and the Messiah, the Lord Jesus Christ brings with Him and His coming all the promises of the Father , the Lord God Almighty attached to

276

both. As the anointed One and the Messiah the Lord Jesus Christ was certainly the One who was greater than King David and also the One who continued his lineage as well amongst the people of the Lord ..

277

God Almighty. As
you would
remember the Kings
of Israel were the
ones who anointed
by the Prophets of
the people of the
Lord God Almighty
with oil. Here was
the Lord Jesus who

also was the anointed One , except that he Himself had been anointed by His Father, the Lord God Almighty. As the very Son of God, He did not need to be anointed by a man?

He had already been anointed by his Father for the mission and the reason why the Father sent Him to the earth. All of which points to the Kingly aspects of the Lord Jesus Christ being the ' Christ ' of

God; the One who had been anointed by the Father, the Lord God Almighty. It is also interesting to think about the fact as the anointed One , the Lord Jesus Christ had been set apart by his Father, the Lord God Almighty. He had been set apart for a purpose, task and mission by His Father, the Lord God Almighty. All of which fits with the concept of Salvation History and the very reality that the Lord Jesus Christ plays and played a very important role in it's fulfillment and consummation in terms of humanity - at - large?

Finally, as the

One who is and was and will be the 'Christ' of the Lord God Almighty, He is the One we want people to accept as we share the Good News of the Gospel with them. In the end, one has to see and accept that the Lord Jesus Christ was in reality the true 'Christ' of the Father, the Lord God Almighty, to become 'Born Again' in Him and through Him. All of which why the Name ' Christ' is so important !

285

286

287

288

289

290

292

293

294

295

7.

SON OF GOD :

As we begin this chapter, it is worth noting that even the Devil recognizes that the Lord Jesus Christ is in reality ' the Son of God ?' A lot hinges on whether or not you believe that the

Lord Jesus Christ is the Son of God? To receive Him into your own life you need to come to a point where you believe this to be true of the Lord Jesus Christ Himself. Everything depends upon this

298

being the truth about the Lord Jesus Christ. He is either truly the very Son of God or He is not the Son of God? I know what I believe and that is that, he truly is the Son of God. This is in part , why this book exists ; I want you to come to see the Diamond that the Lord Jesus Christ was, is and will be as the very Son of God? It is this question that one needs to make their own mind up about; was and is the Lord Jesus Christ, the very Son of God. If you answer yes to this question then you need to come humbly before Him and accept Him into your own life or if you decide otherwise ,

301

then you can
disregard Him?

The writer's of
the various Gospels
saw the Lord Jesus
Christ as the very
Son of God; this is in
part why they wrote
their Gospels about
His life and times? As

302

the very Son of the Living God, He did all these amazing miracles and other mighty acts as chronicled in the Gospel accounts themselves.

It's also worth noting that the

Lord Jesus Christ self - identified as being the One who was the very Son of God; as per John 11 : 4? Throughout His whole life the Lord Jesus Christ had the very awareness that He was in reality the very Son of God. All of which is the basis on which He constantly throughout the Gospel accounts prays to the Father, the Lord God Almighty; His Father as the very Son of the Living God. In the end, it is reasonable to put a lot of weight and substance on the way the Lord Jesus Christ viewed Himself as being the very Son of the Living Lord God Almighty? Because in the end, His own self - identification as the very Son of the Living Lord God Almighty colored everything He did, said and all that happened and took place in His life and times upon the earth.

When one invokes and declares the very name of the Lord Jesus Christ as truly being the Son of God; then one is invoking and declaring the divine

308

into the situation and circumstance of one's life. This is why it is so important to attest to the very reality of one of the Names of the Lord Jesus Christ being the very Son of God ?

Also, it is so important to note that the Lord Jesus Christ has to fully be the Son of God to be all that He was required to be for all of humanity by His Father in Heaven. He cannot just be partly the very Son of God; He has to be fully the Son of God? If He was not fully the Son of God, then He cannot be the Incarnation of the Lord God Almighty come to all humanity and for it as well.

311

The bottom -
line , is in the end, if
He were not fully the
very Son of God
become Incarnate as
a human being, then
there is no way He
could have saved us
and done the very

miracles from the Lord God Almighty that it is said He did in the Gospel accounts? In the end, I would hope that you can see from all of this why it is so important to attest to Him being the Son of God?

313

314

315

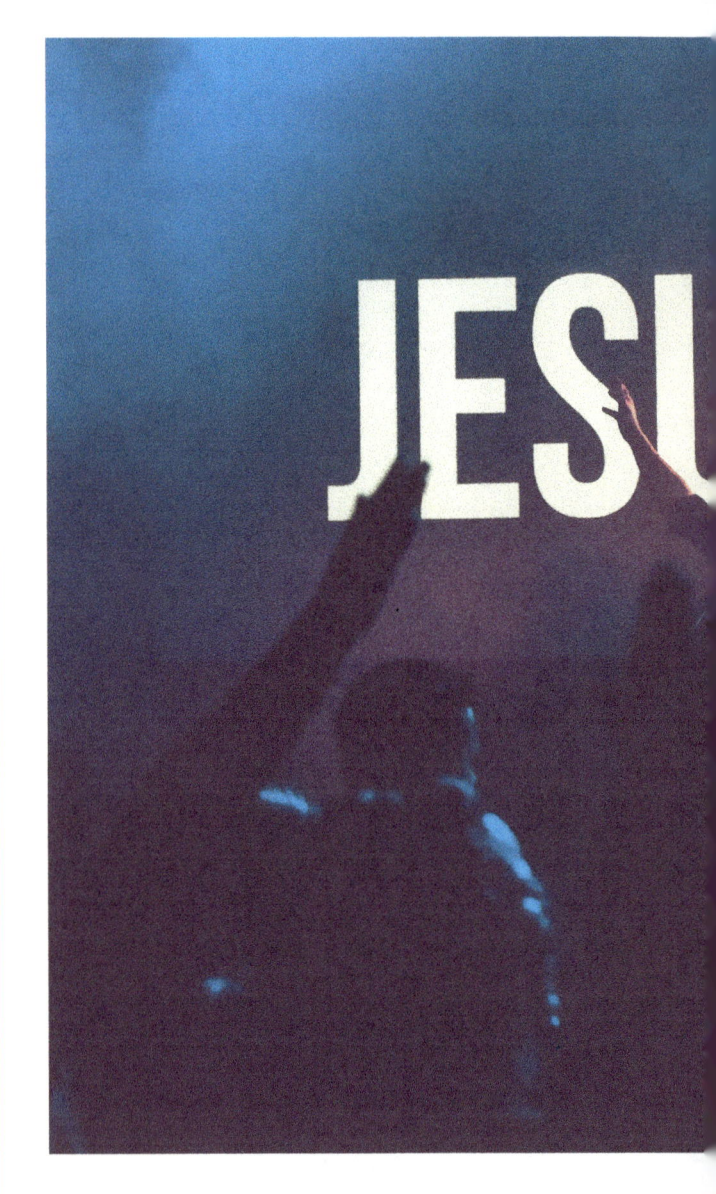

316

317

318

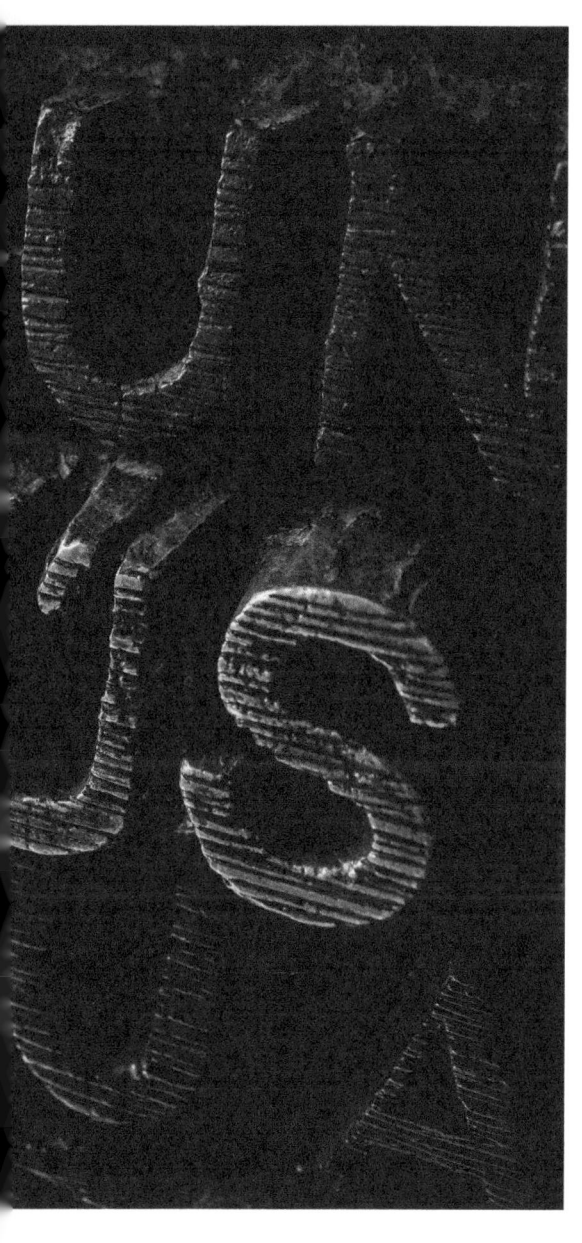

319

8.

SON OF

MAN :

Just so you know we are now going to consider the Name of the Lord Jesus Christ as the ' Son of Man?' In part because this is the other bookend to the Son of God? In

the end, for the Lord
Jesus Christ to fully
seen and appreciated
for who he was, is
and will be He has to
have both nature's
fully; both that of God
and that of Man? In
the end, the
theological construct

322

regarding the Lord Jesus Christ being both fully god and fully Man does not hold true and as a valid if He is deficient in either nature and it's being full - blown in Him? The simple reality, is that, it is because He was fully the Son of Man that he can and does and will identify fully with us all as human beings and part of Mankind. If He had been just fully the Son of God then He

would not and will not
be able to identify
fully with us as
human beings and as
part of Mankind.
Therefore, it is so
very important that
we hold fast to the
reality of the Lord
Jesus Christ being ..

fully the Son of Man. To downplay this part of His very nature is to lose His humanity and human nature and means of identifying with us fully as human beings. We need to keep the very tension in place between the two natures of the Lord Jesus Christ, the Divine on the one hand and the Human on the other hand.

He does all the miracles and other things as a human being operating in the power, authority and unction of the Holy Spirit, the third person of the trinity, who was and is Himself the Lord ...

328

God Almighty. All of which can and should give us real hope, faith and even a belief that we too can operate in similar ways with the very unction of the power of the Holy Spirit in our lives and through them . Clearly, we are ourselves are not the 'Christ' or the Son of God and yet He did say that we would do greater things than He Himself had done upon the earth by and through the

330

very unction and empowerment of the Holy Spirit Himself. All of which is why it is so important to see the Lord Jesus Christ as the Son of Man; fully a human being and as a having a human nature?

331

332

333

334

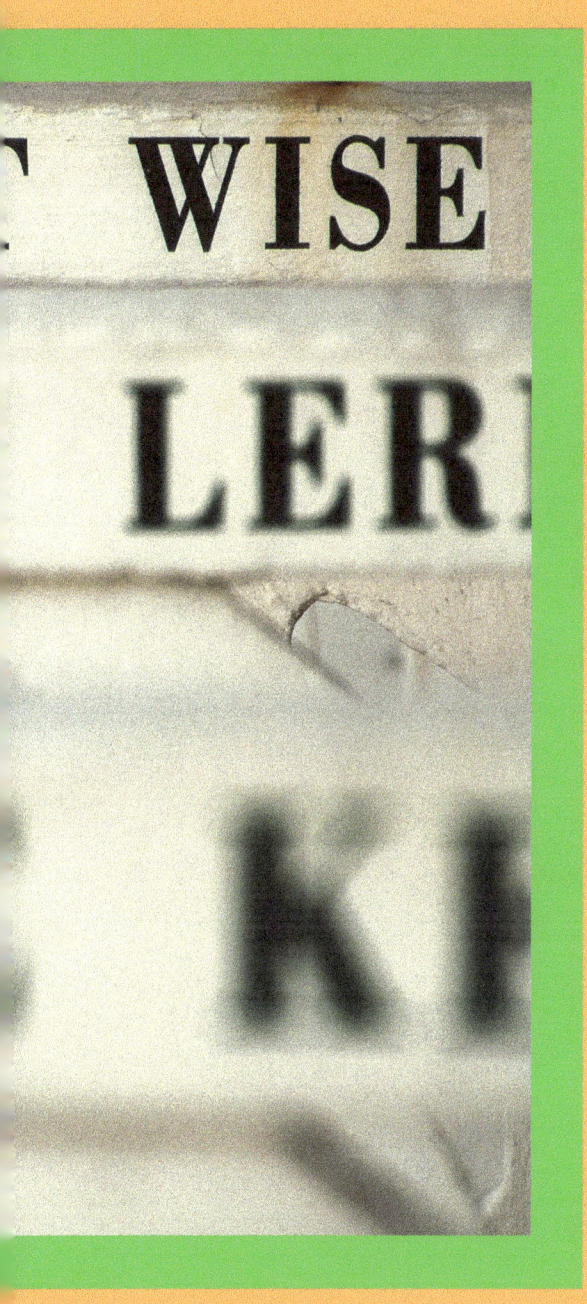

335

336

337

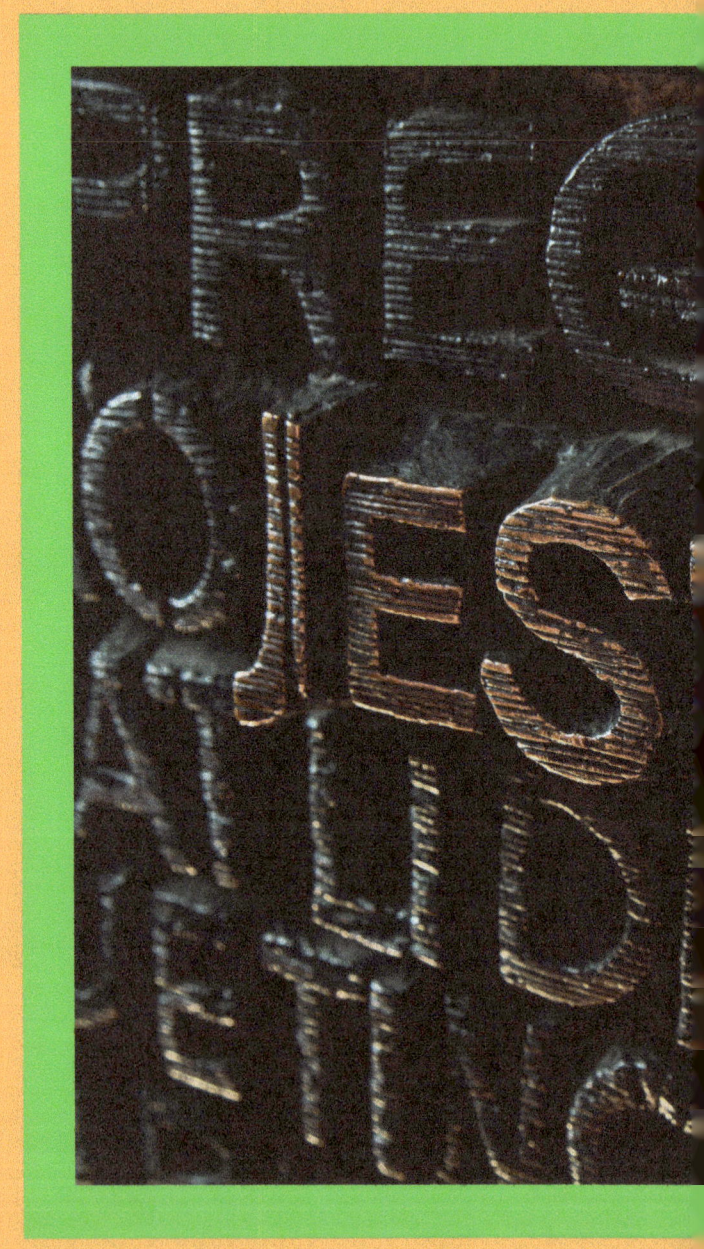

338

339

341

342

9.

LAMB
OF GOD :

This is the very Name that John the Baptist gave to the Lord Jesus Christ, right at the beginning of His ministry to the people of the Lord God Almighty, Israel and humanity - at - large to some extent?

345

This Name that the Lord Jesus Christ is called by John the Baptist brings to our minds the Letter to the Hebrews and it's imagery and images of sacrifice of the Lord Jesus Christ. It

346

brings to our minds the notion that the Lord Jesus Christ through His own death upon the Cross of Calvary was and is the perfect sacrifice for the sins and wrongdoing of all humanity to the Lord

347

God Almighty, the Father, His Father as the very Son of God.

It's interesting that this Name is invoked by John the Baptist at the very beginning of the ministry of the Lord

348

Jesus Christ, in that, it also is a Name that colors the whole of His earthly ministry as well as the other Names we have dealt with in this very book.

By the Lord Jesus Christ knowing and self - identifying as the very Lamb of God; one can see clearly that he had foreknowledge of what His own fate would be regarding the Cross of Calvary. As the very One who was to be the Lamb of God; He knew that He would ultimately die upon a Roman Cross by Crucifixion for the wrongdoing of all humanity. The perfect, once and for all sacrifice for all the wrongdoing of all humanity - at - large. This point, is important to see that there does not need to be anymore ...

352

sacrifices made by humanity - at - large; His was the perfect and the one and only sacrifice that was required by the Father, the Lord God Almighty. All of which does away with people and ....

their needs and desires to continually make sacrifices to cover their own and the wrongdoings of others? Which is why in end, the Lord Jesus Christ was rightly seen by John the Baptist as the Lamb of God who takes away the wrongdoing and the very sins of the world? Which is why it is so important to see the Lord Jesus Christ as the Lamb of God?

358

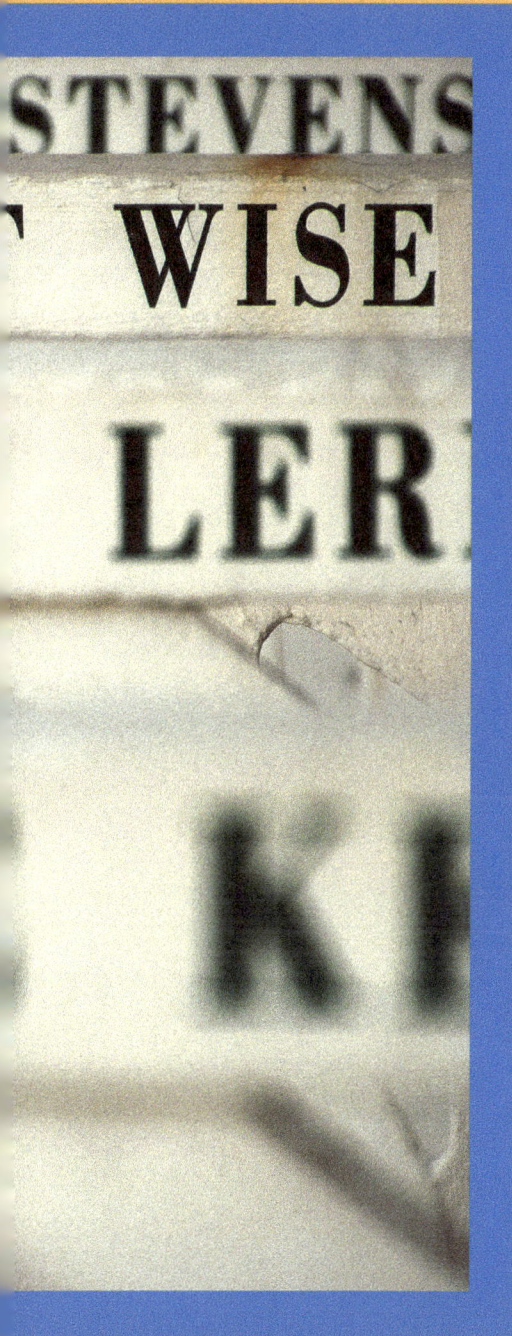

359

360

361

362

363

364

365

366

367

10.

MESSIAH :

We will
consider the Name
of the Lord Jesus
Christ as 'Messiah?'
The word 'Messiah'
has particular
meanings for the
people of the Lord

369

God Almighty; Israel and the Jewish Faith and People of the times of the Lord Jesus Christ. In many ways, the very One who was 'Messiah' was the One who had been foretold as coming from the Lord God Almighty by the Prophets and the very Scriptures. The people of the Lord God Almighty were awaiting the appearance of this One. With the very coming and appearance of the Lord Jesus Christ the 'Messiah' had come and has come and will come again, in terms of His Second Coming to earth , as has been foretold in the very Word of God, the Scriptures Old and New Testament's? As we can see from our readings of the Gospel accounts there were some of the people of the Lord God Almighty ..

who truly believed
that the Lord Jesus
Christ was rightly
the One True
Messiah who had
come from the
Father, the Lord
God Almighty. At the
same time; there
were those who in

no way could ever accept that a son of Joseph the Carpenter from Nazareth in Galilee could ever be the Messiah come to them from the Lord God Almighty?

      It is so very

important to see the Lord Jesus Christ as the One, true and valid Messiah come from the Father, the Lord God Almighty. Because in the end, as this Messiah He was the One who ...

had been prophesied about in the Word of God, the Scriptures. It in the end, it's all caught up with the Word of God being the truth about the Lord God Almighty. The Lord Jesus ..

377

Christ needs to be the One and true Messiah come from the Father, the Lord God Almighty for the whole of the Word of God to be both truth and to hold together and be the coherent Word of God for all humanity to read and come to an acceptance of.

Finally, the Lord Jesus Christ as seeing him as the Messiah who had come from the Father , adds to our understanding and

comprehension of
the Diamond that is
the Lord Jesus Christ
in plain and full
splendor and view.
Our understanding of
the Lord Jesus Christ
is diminished if we
do not correctly see
Him as being the ...

380

One who, is and will be the One and true Messiah of the Lord God Almighty. The Messiah promised of Old has come and has lived, ministered and died and been resurrected again in the Lord Jesus Christ!

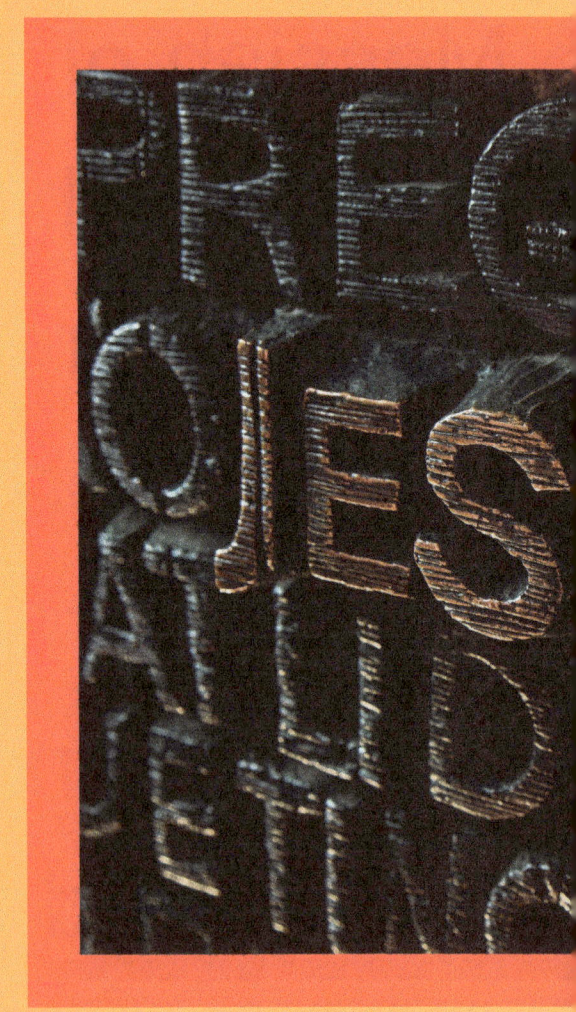

382

383

384

385

387

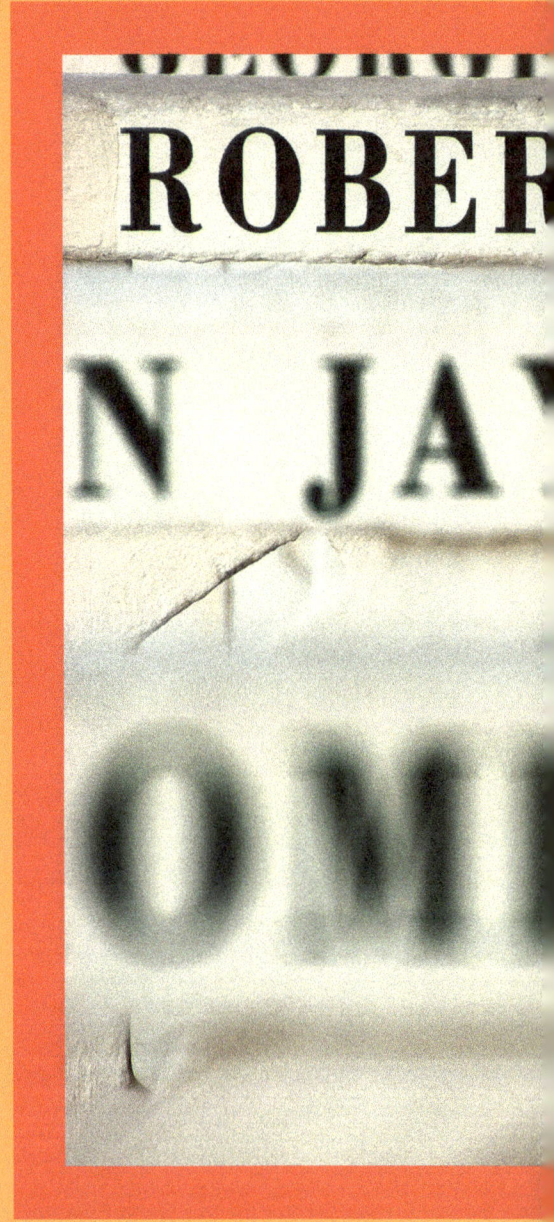

388

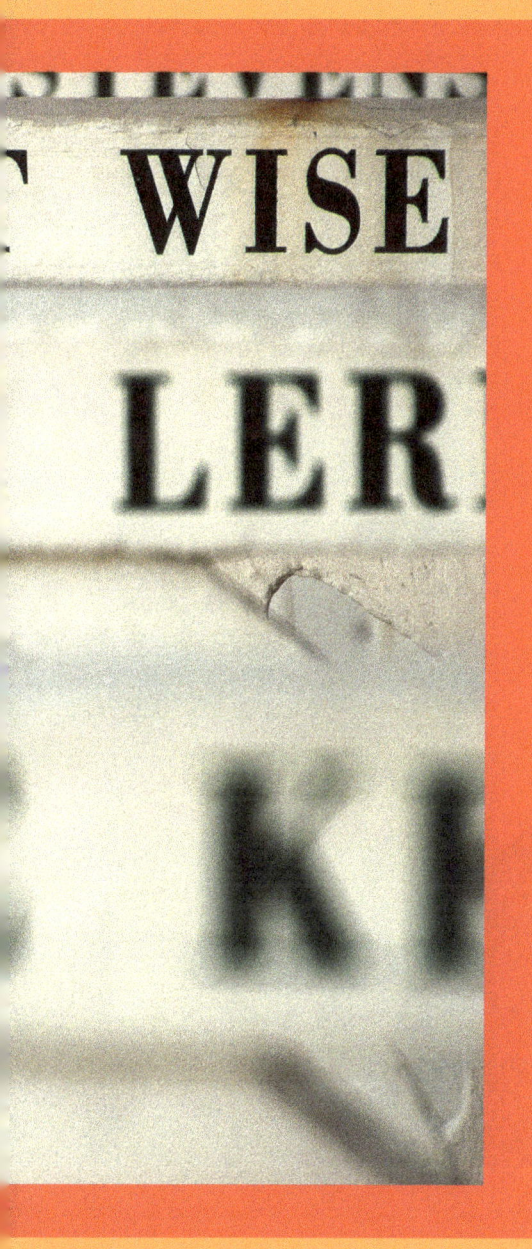

390

391

11.

" I AM "
STATEMENTS
IN JOHN'S
GOSPEL :

392

This is quite
rightly the second last
chapter of this book
entitled ' Name The
Name Of Jesus ?' What
the Lord Jesus Christ
Himself does through
his very ' 1 AM '
Statements in the Gospel
of John adds
considerably to our own

understanding of the Names of the Lord Jesus Christ. Each 'I AM' statement adds and mounts up the information and revelation to do with the very Names of the Lord Jesus Christ? One cannot read and reflect upon these very statements without ...

coming face to face with the Lord Jesus Christ revealed in the Gospel of John in all His glory, honor and majesty as the Son of God, the Son of Man and the true Lamb of God. Each statement gives a different aspect of who the Lord Jesus Christ was , is and will be in ..

the future , when he returns again to the earth and humanity that He died upon the Cross of Calvary to save from their wrongdoing and themselves as well?

The interesting thing about each of the "1 AM Statements" , is that , they each deal with everyday things, things that were in reality common to the people who made up the audience He was addressing at that particular moment in time and space. All of which these statements resonate with so many people ; even the reader's of the Gospel of John today? We too

get a more fully
developed and full
blown picture of who
the Lord Jesus Christ
was, is and will be as
we read and ponder
these very statements
from the Lord Jesus
Christ Himself. After
reading these " I AM "
statements in John's ..

Gospel one cannot help but to have a greater knowledge and real understanding of what the Lord Jesus Christ was, is and will be all about. In some ways, they tell and inform us all as to the very character of the Lord Jesus Christ and what He came to do ?

399

400

401

402

403

404

405

406

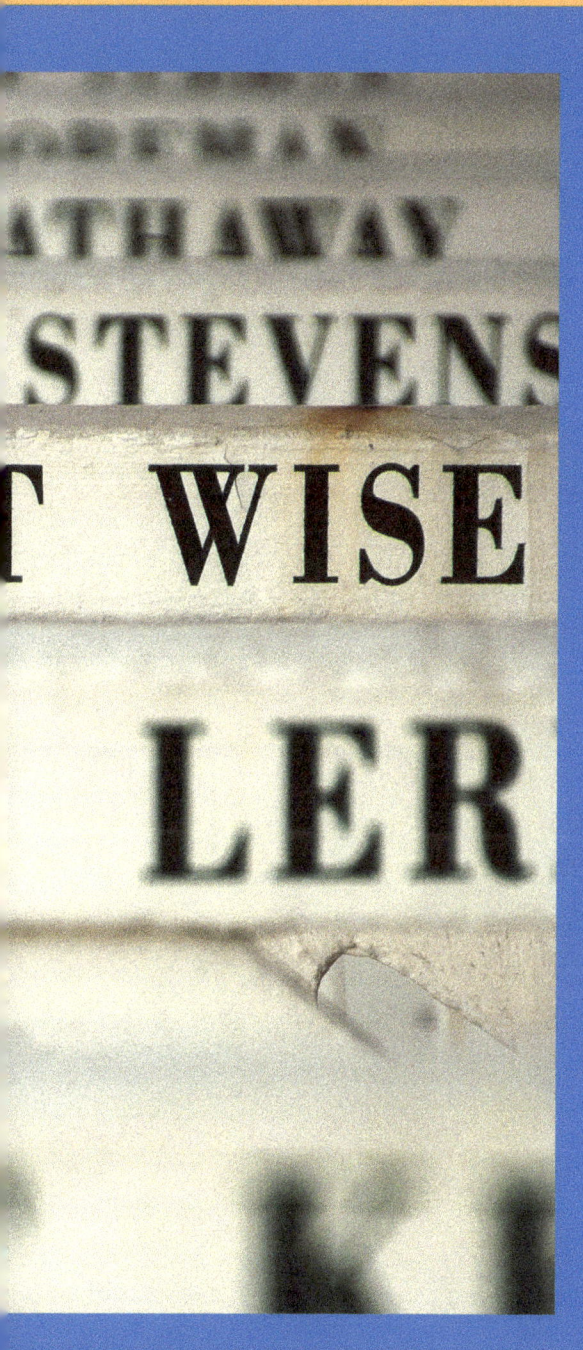

407

12.

EPILOGUE

:

This is the
final chapter of
this book which
has sought to get
us all to think
about the various
Names attached to
the Lord Jesus
Christ and what ..

they mean and their significance to us all? In many ways, trying to understand the Lord Jesus Christ is like trying to view a Diamond , one that is highly valued and worth a lot to many people, even today in our times and in our generations. We have viewed this Diamond through the many and varied Names attached to the Lord Jesus Christ. As we have seen each Name ascribed to Him helps us understand Him

412

in greater ways
and to have a
more balanced
view of the very
Diamond that He
really is! One
should not take
one name by
itself but rather

it is important to give consideration to all the Names ascribed to the Lord Jesus Christ and to therefore view the whole of the Diamond that

He is. My prayer, is that, you now see that there is so much more to the very names ascribed to the Lord Jesus Christ? AMEN !!!

The
Author :

john c Burt

JOHN HAS BEEN A FOLLOWER OF THE LORD JESUS CHRIST; THE VERY LAMB OF GOD , FOR FORTY - THREE YEARS AND STILL GOING STRONG + ALIVE!

418

JOHN LOVES COFFEE, CHICKEN AND CHIPS AND THE ODD HAMBURGER WITH THE LOT ON IT. AS WELL AS CHICKEN AND JELLYFISH !

419

A PRAYER THAT
YOU ALL MIGHT
LIKE TO PRAY IS
AS FOLLOWS:
DEAR LORD
JESUS CHRIST ;
THANK YOU FOR
YOUR COMING TO
THE EARTH ! AND

420

FOR YOUR
SACRIFICE UPON
THE CROSS , EVEN
FOR ME AND FOR
ALL HUMANITY.
HELP ME TO
UNDERSTAND
YOUR NAME ?
AMEN !!!

421

AMEN

AND

AMEN!!!

422

SHALOM :

Lightning Source UK Ltd.
Milton Keynes UK
UKHW020227010820
367490UK00001B/5/J